AF571845

tibia
books

Angela Goldemund, a German-American born in Munich, Germany as the granddaughter of journalist and playwright Josef Maria Jurinek, whom she never met as he had died under mysterious circumstances in 1940, lives in a gray farmhouse in Virginia with her husband and two gray cats. She earned a Ph.D. from the University of Munich and continued her post-graduate studies in theology, liturgy and philosophy at Georgetown University in Washington, DC. Working in various professional fields over the past thirty years, she shed names and disciplinary approaches yet remained truthful to her ultimate calling to be a messenger.

As an editor and scholarly writer, she midwifed ideas on foreign-language training and cultural education; as an art teacher and performance artist, she created environments for aesthetic experiences. As a poet, she strings together a mysterious necklace of sorrowful, joyful and beautiful words and images, a symbol of humanity.

The Gray Notebook of a Stranger

A Poetic Breviary for Seekers

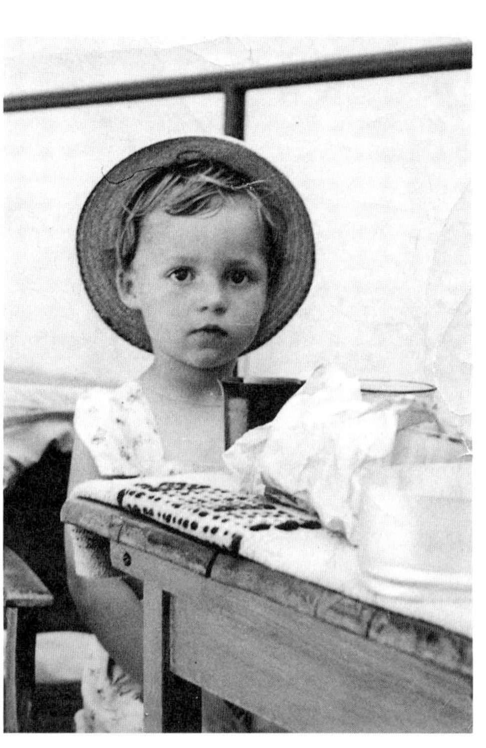

The Gray Notebook Of A Stranger

Angela Goldemund

tibia books P.O. Box 2383 Alexandria, Virginia 22301, USA

Book design by Deborah Dixon Pawlik
Photograph by Herbert Jurinek, Sr.

The Goetz Printing Company
Printed in the United States

ISBN 0–9723749–0–6

To the Living and the Dead

In memory of
Franziska Goldemund

Some who live are dead
and some who are dead
still alive

Philo Judaeus

Contents

Foreword

How often have Angela Goldemund and I shared our wrenching concerns about the new, perhaps darker world we have entered since the monstrous events of September 11. The words 'new world' have fallen from our lips repeatedly. So many things came to mind in the months following the tragedy, things echoed in our public discourse: How much have our lives changed? How may we protect ourselves? Whom can we trust? Are our authorities able to cope? Will we be able to escape future attacks? All these questions recurred in our minds with poignancy every time we passed the Pentagon building with its gaping mouth of a hole and its charred black lips. Are there escape routes? But from what would we be escaping? A biological attack? Suicide bombers? A general panic? Perhaps ultimately from our humanity since the drive to escape fosters an every-man-for-himself mindset. Escape as escapism?

The poetry contained herein calls, as all poetry should, for reflection and self-reflection – to look into the mirror which the poet holds up to us. The mirror's reflections ask us to recognize not so much what is different about the world since September 11 but what transcends the horror of that day, what is timeless and universal about the human condition. Not all the poems here deal with September 11; some were written earlier, others well afterwards, with the event not immediately in mind. But the themes of Angela Goldemund's poetic voice are universal and differ little from those that affected humanity when Agamemnon, Achilles, and Odysseus laid siege to Troy. Those themes – life, death, love, truth, courage, freedom, fear, jealousy, hate, covetousness, and hubris, among others – affect us today as they did our ancient forebears. This may be the ultimate message in these offerings; they stir up our minds and touch the core of our being. The themes are many, but ultimately they are few and universal – fate, humanity and the need for perspective.

Angela Goldemund is also writing about modernity, or the modern world – or perhaps, better said, what has happened to the world of our youth. Our contemporary world is changing at a lightning pace, producing an indigestable volume of information, and our minds are jammed with data – about investments, mortgage interest rates, medical bills, how to build a home addition, the best schools for our children. We know so much about so many things, but in times of crisis we seem to understand so little. The tragedy like the one that occurred on September 11 appeared at first to make us forget our information-glutted and money-obsessed lives, but it was not long before disputes over government-financed compensation for the families of the victims began to arise – who gets how much, a theme raised in the poem *The Dead Won't Cry.*

The poems here are meant to bring us away from such ephemeral issues and to provide the reader some guidance on matters important to the human condition but without making judgements for us. They merely ask that we engage our powers of association to stimulate thoughts and feelings. Rather than filling a sheet full of information, written to explicate or direct, the poet drops a few words onto a page, leaving much white space. The white space allows us to breathe and free ourselves from the yoke of information excess. The poet asks us to step back and use the few offered words as guideposts in helping us to find our own way through the chaos we call life.

Angela Goldemund has chosen to speak in her two languages, German and English – the voices of her life. She calls herself a stranger who straddles cultural borders. As an American, she looks at her German past. As a German, she contemplates her American present. She weaves past and present together in the intricate fabric of a poetic life. Thus, German and English poems are interwoven here with one another rather than presented in two distinct sections. The writer offers few translations; she rather invites readers to reach out to one another to bridge language and cultural barriers through dialogue. Thus, poems become facilitators of mutual understanding.

Why a 'Gray Notebook'? At first glance, gray seems to represent the ashes and dust of destruction such as what we witnessed in the aftermath of the attacks on the World Trade Center in New York and the Pentagon in Washington – the ashes of both the terrorists and the victims. Gray seems to signify little else except perhaps a quality of 'in between': between black and white, good and evil, birth and death, love and hate. Does gray suggest the ambivalence of life's realities?

Perhaps the ultimate theme of these poems is the individual's search for redemption, not in the narrow sense of having one's sins expiated – rather of personal liberation from all that is artificial, ephemeral, from all that makes us a stranger to ourselves and others. Angela Goldemund holds up her poetic mirror not only to us but also to herself. And here is an irony, that becoming less of a stranger to oneself may mean becoming more of a stranger to one's environment, straddling the border of the pragmatic and spiritual worlds.

I hope that readers will find the time spent with these poetic reflections rewarding.

—George Goldemund

Vorwort

"Den ersten Schmerz trägt man wie einen Magneten in seinem Herzen, weil alle Zärtlichkeit von dort ausstrahlt", schrieb die amerikanische Schriftstellerin Jane Bowles. Den ersten Schmerz in seinen vielfältigen Erscheinungsformen, ihn beschwört Angela Goldemund in ihrem ersten Gedichtband. Da ist der allererste, vernichtende Schmerz, den ein weibliches Kind erfährt, wenn die Mutter in Klage über seine Geburt ausbricht. *(I wondered / who you would be / but you had dreamed / who I should be ... / a boy!)* Da ist der Urschmerz der Seele, die, in einem Fleischhemd, in eine Welt der Verlassenheit, des materiellen Verhaftetseins, des Todes geworfen ist. *(Answers whirl round the earth./ The abyss works all by itself.)* Und da ist der neue Schmerz, der schockartig angesichts einer kollektiven Katastrophe überfällt. *(Ihre Söhne sind verbrannt. / Auf dem Türstock stehen / in weißer Kreide / geschrieben / keine Namen. / 11.9.2001.)*

Anders als die unbewußte Mehrheit sperrt Angela Goldemund diesen Schmerz nicht in eine Kammer des Vergessens ein. Im Sinne Joseph Beuys' zeigt sie ihre Wunde. Sie trägt den Schmerz in ihrem Herzen, innig, wie eine Kostbarkeit. Und so strahlt alle Zärtlichkeit, alle Intensität, alles Leben, alle Passion, alle Sinnlichkeit, alle Spiritualität von diesem Schmerz aus. Ihre Gedichte sind Klagelieder, Trauergesänge, – doch sie sind auch Anrufung, Gebet, Vision, Entzücken. Bilder aus den Tiefen der Psyche, die hinüberweisen in eine spirituelle Welt der Erlösung, ohne den irdischen, sinnlichen Grund, aus dem alle Kunst erwächst, zu verlassen. So entsteht Ganzheit, eine Balance zwischen Schwerkraft und Leichtkraft – der Ort des eigentlich Menschlichen.

Eine Künstlerin entdeckt sich als Lyrikerin. Sprachwelten schieben sich über Bilderwelten, durchdringen sie mit Bewußtsein, geben ihnen Klang. Doch Sprachwelten stoßen auch an Grenzen, an Verständigungs-, an Landesgrenzen, und hier lag die besondere Herausforderung für Angela Goldemund, die, beheimatet im bayrischen Deutschland, nach Amerika ausgewandert ist und seit vielen Jahren in der Nähe von Washington, DC lebt. Ihre Gedichte sind zweisprachig, wie sie selbst, und doch entstand für mich, die mit der gleichen Zweisprachigkeit lebt, beim Lesen ein paradoxes Phänomen: Ich wußte nach der Lektüre eines Gedichts nicht mehr, ob es in Englisch oder in Deutsch geschrieben war: Das Medium Sprache, scheinbar von so großer Bedeutung beim Schreiben, entpuppt sich als Fleischhemd, das mit Leichtigkeit abgestreift werden kann. Eine dritte Sprache, die Sprache der Seele tritt machtvoll in Erscheinung. Das lyrische Ich ist hier nicht (sprachgebundenes) Individuum, es zeigt sich als Archetyp: "The Ancient One", die weise, zeternde, und doch immer neu gebärende, machtvolle *grauäugige Alte* unseres kollektiven Unbewußten.

Einige Leser werden die Performance-Künstlerin in diesen Texten wiederentdecken: Angela Goldemund kreiert Raum in ihren Gedichten, setzt oft Figuren, Gegenstände, Gefühle in diesen leeren Raum und scheint lediglich zu beobachten, welche Sprachreaktionen entstehen. *(Porzellanweiß / schön zurechtgemacht / zwischen makellosen Tüchern / eingebettet.)* Andere werden der Bedeutung graphischer Formen im Text nachspüren wollen. Alle aber lädt dieser Gedichtband in einen Raum der Kontemplation ein. Was wäre wichtiger in unruhiger Zeit?

—Carna Zacharias

Und Sprich
And Speak

Und Sprich Grauäugige Alte

eingekerkert
im Herzen unter Schmerzen
in der Tiefe begraben ...

bis die Raben kamen
kreischten und keiften
der Wind über die Weite pfeifte
die Wasser gegen die Mauern peitschten
bis es bebte
und sich die graugrüne Raupe
aufs neue verpuppte
verwandelte
zum Schmetterling wurde
und flog
flog übers Meer –

komm und
laß dich erkennen.
Steig aus der goldenen Höhle
deiner ewigen Augen ans Licht
und sprich.

Ich werde dich erinnern ...
Sei gegrüßt.

And Speak Gray-Eyed Old Woman

imprisoned within
writhing with pain
buried deep down ...

until the ravens came
screeched and shrieked
until sharp winds swept across the land
and waters lashed against the wharves
until it quaked
the gray-green larva burst
cocooned itself until
it spread its wings
transformed
and flew as butterfly
flew across the sea –

come and
let me see you.
Leave the golden reefs of your
everlasting eyes, be revealed
and speak.

I shall remember you ...
Hail to you.

Come To Me

Come to me and show
me your wound.
Tell me how they wove
you into the spoked wheel
since you'd smashed their idols.

Come to me and speak
of your pain.
Tell me how they stripped off
your clothes and pierced your eyes
since you'd laid them bare.

Come to me and cast off
your flesh.
Lay down close to me
as you did in foretimes.
Let me taste
who you are.

Fleischhemd

Ihr Fleisch an Knochen
angebunden, tief zerschunden
ist noch nicht restlos überwunden.

Einst war es ihnen auf die Reise
mitgegeben, sich ins Dieseits einzuleben,
sich daraus ein Hemd zu weben.

Die Götter liebten ihre Toten mit Gold
umwoben, ins Dunkel eingeschoben,
für das Jenseits aufgehoben.

Bis dann der eine kam wie Du und Ich,
geboren, wie ein Lamm geschoren,
im Tod dem Fleischhemd abgeschworen.

THEY FOUND

They found a young man
a beautiful man
a naked man
lying face down near the border
arms and legs broken
deep shrapnel wounds
burnt into his back
eyes drained into the earth
a lonely man.

They found a young man
a beautiful man
a naked man
lying near the Sacred Gate
holding up the road
with broken arms
backbone marked
by ancient wheels
a lonely man.

They found a young man
a beautiful man
a dutiful man
lying face up near the exit
arms and legs twisted
around a beam of steel
neck crushed
eyes frozen
a lonely man.

They found a young universe
a beautiful universe
an old universe
breathing and self-birthing
expanding and contracting
radiating new light
a lonely universe
and they said
it is good.

THE DEAD WON'T CRY

The Dead won't cry.
Once it's over
we cry
to feel alive.

Once it's over,
we want to hear their voices
taped - printed - digitized;
it doesn't matter
since they can't say no.

What is a dead man worth today?
He has his price for sure.
How much, d'you know?

Once we were given life for free.
Now we have to pay
for crying our first and last
into infinity.

Can you decipher birth and death?
Can you invent what's in between?
What does the zero really mean?

One says
that zero calls for nothingness?
Not meaningless for sure.
Or zeroes call for covetousness?
Not meaningless for sure.
Choose big, go big
and pick your prize.

And then?

I heard them cry, the Dead
and cried with them.

The Child Woke Up And Cried

They were born and died
in iron coats and arms
frozen to cones of ice
but their tears
kissed the night
with closed eyes
they frayed
and all their fears
hummed inside the heart
the child woke up and cried.

They frayed
in iron coats and arms
but their tears
and all their fears
kissed the night
with closed eyes
the child woke up and cried
hummed inside the heart
frozen to cones of ice
they were born and died.

With closed eyes
the child woke up and cried
and all the fears
kissed the night
they were born and died
they frayed
frozen to cones of ice
in iron coats and arms
but their tears
hummed inside the heart.

Coats and arms
hummed inside
the child
froze to ice
but the tears
and all the fears
woke up and cried
with closed eyes
the iron heart
frayed
kissed the night
was born and died.

Golcuk The Year After

Senem Kus
A deadly kiss embarked you on
your mother's grief,
another summer morn arose,
with cries of love unheard.

Senem Kus
my child
you found your nethermost
in Mother Gaia's land,
wherefrom you rose anew
to thy white pale blue strand.

My child
stretch out your hands
and let me know
when our time will come.
Meanwhile I grieve
and mourn your loss,
my shaken knees bent down.

Golcuk, Turkey was the site of a disastrous earthquake in August 1999.

MUTTERHAUS

Kein Baum erinnert mehr
an die Tollheit jugendlichen
Übermuts und Glücks.

DER LETZTE STURM LEGTE DIE MÜDEN
WURZELN ZUR RUHE.

Der Zaun ist eingerissen.
Die Mauer mußte der Wucht
des Schlages weichen.

DER LETZTE STURM LEGTE DIE MÜDEN
WURZELN ZUR RUHE.

Männer zerhacken die verlorene Zeit
in gleichförmige Kälte.
Frauen schichten die Erinnerungen
auf den Karren der Tränen.

DIE RUINE STEHT STILL.

Kein Baum erinnert mehr
an die Tollheit jugendlichen
Übermuts und Glücks.

KINDER SPIELEN IM GRAS.

Gebet

Vater - Mutter
Wir hörten dich nicht.
Wir berührten dich nicht.
Wir sahen dich nicht.
Wir liebten dich nicht.

Vater - Mutter
Wir blieben im Schlamm
unserer Exkremente stecken,
nach Hilfe rufend, bis es fast
schon zu spät war.

Vater - Mutter
wir hielten uns an unseren
goldenen Kälbern fest, die uns
zogen, nach unten zogen.

Deine Töchter und Söhne
waren dem Wahnsinn nahe,
bis du aus dem Inneren
der Erde riefst:
Ich liebe euch!

Und unsere Tränen verklärten
dein Antlitz voller Schmerzen;
du wurdest zum Schmerzensmann,
an dem wir uns hochziehen konnten.

Amen.

Stossgebet

Löse die Klammern aus meinem Fleischhemd/
ziehe die gefräßigen Maden aus meinem Fett/
gewähre mir den Atem zu verharren/

... / ...

ich horche in den Abgrund

... und ...

es schreit aus ihm herauf:
Hast du mich vergessen?

... ? ...

Ich schreie zurück:
Ich sehe nur grau!

Spring!

Und ... ich sprang.

Metamorphoses

It rumbles and quakes ...
above my head a roaring sound
I freeze and hear the wrathful
thunder speak
my windows shake ...
sky-high above I see a trail of smoke
gray signs onto the blue

And then ...
she spoke

And when ...
they plunged and dove
they left their squares and
cubes with fire on their trails
they spread their arms like lonely
squabs not mastering yet their wings
kicked out of their unruly nests
they shot deep down
below like darts
into the spaceless air
into the gray abyss
on one of those hot summer days.

And then ...
the world stood still and
watched the burning nests
while you, my friend,
turned off the show and left.
You ran into the cave and watched
the shady walls. There was this
ancient man who yielded to the rock
until his shield was pierced and broke
apart by slaying hands

before he changed into a bird
and flew beyond on swan-white wings.

And then ...
you listened to the ancient bard
reciting line by line
the rhythmic sounds of flapping wings
as fledglings left their homes
and mothers' tears fell to the ground
where many swans were born.

And then ...
the fate of many sons was drawn
from dreams and rustling leaves
as long as Pythia's voice did not
grow cold.

But then ...
her sisters' voice was raped and killed
by jealous men who wandered up
and down the fields of angst and hate
with sharpened knives and bombs
in bundled sacks of mindful acts.

And then ...
again the gate of wrath and woe
was flooded red with blood of men
while others sat and mused
the art of war today as then.

And then ...
you saw the wooden horse
transform into a metal plane
break through the walls
of power, wealth and dreams
besieging every man who
was to blame for other times.

And then ...
skies changed

I raise my eyes and look again
as playful tails of wind-filled kites
are stitching golden loops
above, below the tattered clouds.
They glow and flare
within all gray.

Now, Death ...

Shuttered
shattered
shot
shaken
shed
skin
raw

Who was the one
running with a swaddled bundle
on his back?

Who was the one
carrying the swaddled one
in front?

The beautiful hills
are ribbed with gray limestone
in the olive groves
silvered by a gentle breeze.

Shiver.

It stinks,
garbage stinks,
dead flesh stinks.

starlit
sore
sight

Once life said,
Blessed is the fruit of your womb.

Now, Death ...
what is the fruit of your womb?

The Blinded Men

When I was young I was told
the Story of the Blinded Men.

And grandmother would say:

One Day the salmon's flesh will rot
be washed ashore, not touched
by bear or fox; the seagull will not
feed its young and fly away.
Then men will come to cast their bones
yet will not find the truth.
The ice will melt and flood the earth,
the geese won't fly then north,
then caribous won't shake their heads,
woodpeckers will not peck their trees,
then lakes will dry and fish will die
salt waters swallow ravaged lands.
The eyes of men won't see the drake
for pride and greed have blurred their sight.
They'll buzz around like busy gnats
set up in spaceless heights and fall
deep down from high above into
a blackish sea of drowning grayfish men.
The ring around the moon will gray
and then ... the fire of the sun goes out.

[...]

And then grandmother would say:

You were born, my child,
to be the one who sees the signs in gray.
Are you ready to praise the blue and sing?

Weisst Du?

Weißt du, daß ich ein Kristall bin?

Im hitzigen Gefecht empfangen,
versteckt, verschüttet und verborgen,
gewachsen unter hohem Druck,
geformt
als Engelskind gesegnet
ungenormt
bis sich ein Messer und Gewehr
hartkantig, spitz und ungefähr
hat vorgetastet,
bis dann ein Kind in Weiß gebunden
nach allgemeiner Lust und Mär
schrie, schrie und nochmals schrie.

Dann haben sie den Keim
zur Brust genommen, als Brut verwoben,
betastet und bewundert ohne End
gewogen und erzogen, belogen und betrogen,
säulenschlank vergittert um den Kern
der schmerzverkrampft die Fäuste ballte
bis sich im Traum die Zunge rollte, lallte,
die Türe knallte und die Mauer fiel.

Weißt du, daß ich ein Kristall bin?

Erst wenn der Wind in meine Kanten drängt
und sich das Licht in zarten Nischen fängt
beginne ich zu leuchten und zu tanzen,
der Sonne Strahlen auszuschwingen
für alle Engelskinder dieser Welt,
die mit geballten Schmerzensfäusten
ersticken und vereinsamt sind.

Weißt du, daß auch du funkeln kannst?

A Word

A Word
A Moment
A Touch

[...]

A word
that moves you
A moment
that embraces you
A touch
that holds you

Eine Hand Voll

Eine Hand voll
weißer Träume
lockt mich in die Höhle
des schwarzen Panthers.
Er legt sich vor mich
hin und stirbt.
Ich schließe
den warmen
Tod in meine
Arme.

Der Tag graut.

Nine - One - One

Alone
within my walls
four white corners
gray streaks
deep holes
memories
I set my feet
heel to toe
toe to heel
in silence.
Nine - one - one - two - zero - zero - one
I walk
the spiral
the circle
the square
not once
not twice
not thrice
many times
praying
praising
shouting
thanking
begging
abiding
accepting
the maze.
Nine - one - one - two - zero - zero - one

Nine - one - one - two - zero - zero - one
I bow my head
kneel down
crouch
touch
with empty hands
my chest
I rise
breathe in
wander
touch
with bare feet
the ground
I lift my arms
up to the sky
I cry
Three - one - one - two - zero - zero - two
one - one - two
three.
The tears
have soaked the earth
but
not yet quenched the thirsty tongue
of fire
the embers burn
and smile.

Should We Be Afraid?

How comes it

that Abram, the grandfather, was penned in a wagon
heading East to be gassed and burnt?

that Siegfried, the dragon killer, was killed by
the one who knew his one soft spot?

that the woman, the sister, was chosen to be
raped by the ones who were in power?

that the ones who were crammed in a tower
striving up were doomed to jump or burn?

that the fingers and hands and feet without
names were logged up in the book?

Should we be afraid?

Recitations and refrigerators hum
a soothing sound for the living and the dead.
Twenty thousand human parts
wait patiently, unidentified
at the morgue in New York
for Antigone.

Silence

He coiled up
like a snake
afraid
absorbing
the warmth of
a merciful oven.

The guns went cold
when he was three
early in 1945.

The guns fired again
when he was sixty
late in 2001.

This was the morning
of September 11th
when he began
to understand
the silence
in between.

Strangers

They came and stayed
strangers, big, strong men
always smiling and chewing
while talking.

My sister and I stared at their teeth
their tongues shooting
back and forth, fast
hissing pink darts
seeking the bull's-eye
in and out and in and out ...
They played with little parachutes
that burst at once and fell together
then laced their noses and cheeks
like thin worn rags torn to bits
burying their pinkish bubble speech.
We laughed.

They entered our house and stayed.
Blankets and pillows were not enough,
they wanted more.
Father loaded his rifle and went with them
behind the house. Behind the house
they shot a doe, cooked it on a spit
over a fire and tasted strong beer.
But doe and beer were not enough,
they wanted more.

And father showed them the loft
to rest and sleep in sweet hay
dried in summer's heat. They climbed up
and got hot and ...

It was time for my sister and me
to go to bed.
As we climbed up we heard
the strangers sing and laugh and ...
strange, high-pitched giggles teased
their basses. We tittered and laughed,
we sang our round to conquer the angst.

Ein Vogel wollte Hochzeit machen
in dem grünen Walde,
viderallala, viderallala, viderallalalala.
Brautmutter war die Eule, nahm Abschied
mit Geheule,
viderallala, viderallala, viderallalalala.
Der Pfau mit seinem bunten Schwanz,
der führt die Braut zum Hochzeitstanz,
viderallala, videra ... *

[...]

My story is ended here for now.
We all lived happily ever after.

*A birdman goes a-courting in the wooded green, viderallalalala...
The mother of the bride, the owl, bids farewell with a screech,
viderallalalala...
The peacock with his rainbow tail struts proudly to the bridal dance,
viderallalalala... (from a German folk song)

Don't Forget

The Unseen is hunted like a bird
above the clouds
by the bewildered crowd
beneath the sky
fire and sulphur rain upon the earth
to taste and touch the end
and you can hear the cries
for justice and law
for good and evil
for hope and love
they talk about themselves
the smooth-tongued brothers
the sharp-minded brothers
the brothers of hate
the brothers of faith
the sisters of the iron fist
the sisters of the veil
the mothers of martyrs
the fathers of heroes
the children of Adam and Eve
the children of the same one
not begotten but made.

Friends and foes
have scorched the earth
merciless
hungry for the spark.

I know it now.

Don't forget,
men drink blood
yet there is hope.
Don't forget,
there is just one,
the one
Unseen.

The Old Man

Dead
an old seed
buttoned in a gray coat
dead
jumped from the Table
dead
fell and dried up
no one was there
and was found
no one was there
nowhere
dead.

He came from
a dark place
cold, not bigger
than a toilet stall.
He came from
a small town
called Paradise.
He came from
this side and
left for the
other side
alone.

Zum See

Er geht
mit seiner Bahre
zum See;
seit fünfunddreißig Jahren
verhallen seine Schritte
in der Unterwelt.
Das Echo

seiner
inneren Stürme
bleibt un-
beantwortet. Nur wache
Ohren können seine
Donnergötter
hören.

Er lebt
unter der Decke mit
den Ungestümen.
Tage zerfallen in Finsternis ohne
Feuer am Himmel, bis er
die Decke abwirft,
auf er steht,

um erneut
die Bahre zu nehmen,
zum See
zu gehen, dort tief einzutauchen.
Sein Schweigen gleicht zart
perlender, funkelnder
Sternstille.

Erlösung

Sie öffnen und schließen
ihre Münder im Takt
des Augenaufschlags.
Zwei Wesen getrennt
durch Glaswände
durch-strahlte Wesen.

Sie schwimmen und schweben
voreinander nicht miteinander
beständig und ruhelos
in Licht und Wasser
ohne Feuer
ohne Erde

bis es bebt, brennt,
die Glaswände einstürzen und
schmelzen.
Fäuste atmen wie Muscheln
pochen und züngeln
im feurigen Rhythmus.

Sie verschmelzen
untrennbar vereinigt eins
im Sterben.
Nun liegen sie zusammen
zwischen Spiegelwänden
ein Wesen
unzählbar vervielfacht
un-sichtbar.

Noch weiß es keiner,
das Tor zur Kammer
liegt im Schloß,
der Schlüssel ist
versteckt.

Der Kirschstein

Die weiße Made frißt sich durch
das blutrote Kirschenfleisch
eifrig und emsig
bis sie sich fett und müde
zusammenrollt und schläft
auf ein Wunder wartet.

Der Kern bleibt dem Wurm
ein dunkles Geheimnis;
seine Werkzeuge
durchdringen ihn nicht.

Der Wanderer pflügt und erntet
ehrgeizig und unbarmherzig
beißt er sich ins noch warme
Fruchtfleisch
labt sich am blutigen
Kirschensaft
trinkt unbewußt
legt sich zur Ruhe.

Die Steine speit er aus:
zu harte Nebensächlichkeiten!
Unbemerkt und unbezweckt
liegen sie im Fall verteilt
sinken langsam aber stetig
mit den Wassern in die Erde.

Die jungen Mädchen singen
und tanzen im Reigen
unter dem Kirschlorbeer
mit kirschgeschmückten Ohren;
leuchtende Kirschmünder
trinken vom delphischen Quell;
Pythische Orgien um den Stein.

Der Stein bricht auf in feuchtwarmer
Umerdung, wenn der Sproß
durch die zarte Krume sticht
ans Licht will
blühen
weiß nicht
warum.

The Call

Call him Mohammed, the young man
riding the bus downtown.
It is his last bus ride.
He is leaving home to arrive.
He will never come back.
They bid him farewell.
His mother cooks his favorite meal,
kebab and cucumber salad, and kisses
his forehead. His father closes the eyes
of his son with a gentle touch and lets him go.
Then Mohammed jumps on the bus.
His younger brother Wusam is already waiting
in line for the next bus to take.

Mohammed dreams of the rose of Sharon
beneath which he had once lain in the shade
drinking from his mother's breasts
smelling the sweetness of almonds.
His heart is filled with love and tenderness.
How beautiful you are, my love,
and how you delight my eyes.
says the voice of his singing heart.
Raising his eyes he sees her, the veiled one,
the virgin who will be espoused to him.
She walks among the busy crowd downtown,
there she is ...
her hand reaches for the white rose
with its feathery, blood-red streaks...
she breaks the rose and gazes at it as if
it were a precious stone reflecting the
light of her eyes radiating through the veil.
He shivers.
Who are you, loveliest of all women?
Are you the one who will be mine?
My heart is yours and yours is mine.

Come, let us wander through the garden of delight.
I will never leave you.
Come then, my beloved.

And then it happened,
his heart embracing the song of love,
the moment of revelation, the bang, the big bang.
The furnace of hate opened its devouring mouth
and swallowed flying
arms and legs,
burnt flesh,
glass shattered to splinters.

Mohammed was nineteen years old
pregnant with fire
pregnant with dynamite
pregnant with death
giving birth to the call.

Who was he whom they called Mohammed?
Who gave up his life full of hate
and dreamed of love?

Answers whirl round the earth.
The abyss works all by itself.

Call 911

Why are you hanging in the closet, little boy?

Ma'am, don't you smell it?
I am dead, I stink.
They tied me up, beat me, slaughtered me.

My life was short.
I was thirteen.
My name is not important.

They wanted to see and feel
what it was like, you know,
to kill.

They were tired of watching movies
just seeing and imagining the stuff;
they needed a hands-on experience,
the real thing.

They wanted to feel the bull's horns
but they didn't know how.
They didn't know about
the runners and
the gored
of
the place
where
the sun rises.
They were simple
don't-care freaks.
Could you do me a favor?

Go down to the garbage bin park.
My sister lives there with her babies.
Take some sandwiches and water to her.

They are hungry.
She was evicted; they threw her out of
the window, her appartment in the tower.
But no one was there to watch it.

If you can't find her, call 911 and
ask them whether they have some
change for her and the kids

maybe from the 911 Fund.

Thanks, ma'am.

Let me take you down, little boy, I will bury you.

Brother

Brother, is this the place of all places?

Who knows, but never go back.

Brother, I have a precious gift tied to myself.
Tell me what you know. It is urgent.

I don't understand you, but be aware of the evil.
It is out there.

Brother, you don't listen. Your ears are clogged.
I carry the Truth under my heart.

You are a dreamer; you are not real.
How can you say this?
The Truth does not exist, there are only data and facts,
or fiction.

Brother, be aware.
I am a messenger of the divine roar.
The Truth will blow you up. I hate you.

Yes, you are a true dreamer. I know that for sure.

Brother, I'll shed blood onto the path of the Truth.
I am building a memorial of invisible power,
of everlasting memories.
Be aware. I am a martyr.

My world works as precise as a clockwork.
I look towards the future and not the past.
I am a true survivor.
When the alarm goes off, I duck and cover.
I have everything under control.
You will taste death first ...

Brother, I will take you all with me. Don't forget,
I follow the Truth.
Living means more than surviving.

The truth is that cars will be scattered on rooftops;
smiling children will be torn in half; burnt flesh
will melt into blood-stained shirt shreds and paint
the scorched earth red.

Brother, your ears are clogged ...

Who are you, calling me Brother?
I am not your brother.
You are an insane victim of illusions, a radical killer,
a trained executioner.

I am a spokesman of the Law, Brother.
I follow the Truth.

Who has appointed you to speak in the name
of the Law. Whose Law?

Brother, words miss the answer.

I see your eyes rolling back into the dark cavern
of your skull; I see your hate.
I see you burning.

... *it's too late ... my blood speaks the ...*

... You are ... you are ...
my blood ...

B-R-O-K-E-N

I am b-r-o-k-e-n,
out of order,
call it dis-order.

Let's give you CC,
you say,
Cash and Counseling.

I want ... to be alone
hold my pain –
not in my brain.

Pet your cat,
you say,
pull the blanket over your ears.

But ...

I don't have time!
They can't give me time off
at this point in time.

Grandmother is dead;
she can't talk to me anymore.
I miss grandpa's kisses und hugs;
he's gone as well.

Our mummies are dead,
our daddies are gone.
We are orphans and lie awake.
We cry and don't fake.
Who needs to know our name?
Who is the one beyond all blame?

Yet ...

We must bounce back,
not worry the others
and wear our slacks.

All hands are busy, all minds at work.
Look for the answer in the pouch of the
clerk: post-disaster psychiatric disorder.

I am assessed, synchronized, sedated!
I am dangerous for
I invite death into your homes.

Can you see the shards,
the shards of my life
on the ground while
meeting and kidding
knitting and netting
necking and checking?

The emergency assistance
business answers the phone:
Good morning, how are you?
What are your symptoms?

I fell out the window ...

The hallways are long,
the windows are shut,
all days have twenty-four hours,
onethousandandfourhundredandforty-
four minutes ...

How often did you fall out the window?

Just once today.
Didn't you hear the sound?
Something has b-r-o-k-e-n.
It wasn't the trellis below the window?
No, but the chains around my heart.

A typical case of emotional fallout.
Room 911. What's your social sec... ?

My shards don't match symptoms ...

Sons Say

I
One Son says

I saw him flip
over his shoulder
I just kinda stood there
I was frozen, like a ...
They punched and kicked
head to head, fist against fist
Quickly, on the ground, three times.
I yelled out:
Stop it! Stop it!
They did not hear me.
Then ...
He was dead.
My father walked away.

II
Another Son says

You riddle too much over facts:
I am
15-year-old
male
pilot
troubled loner
Accutane taker
suicide candidate
suicide note in my pocket.
You
found me dead
my plane crashed
into the 28th floor
of a skyscraper
Bank of America
Ay

But your eyes didn't see me
the boy who spread
his wings
the lonely lover
who fled his prison
of concrete and hate
I was a
neophyte to the sun
and burnt by the sun
like Icarus
the son of Daedalus
who built the labyrinth
and escaped with his son
whose feathers caught fire
before he fell deep
depression
destiny
gray
Ay

III
Other Sons say

Wounded but strong
hungry but alive
caught in fire
we are free.
We are
no prisoners
no pill takers
our spirits are
not weak or tamed.
We are
living candles
fireworks
in the sky
Allah is Great.

We are free
in the fire
hungry but strong
wounded but alive.

IV

And the Daughter says

When life conquered death
light conquered the dark
and the infant universe
gave birth to
space and time
the stars
bright and white
like milk.

And she says

You come from
this milk as
you come from
your mother's
and father's.

And she says

There is light
and
it is good!
Close your eyes
trust and see.
Touch the ground
and sing
a longing song
far away yet near.
Sing!

In Times Of War

Standing on the bridge
late in the afternoon
on an ordinary day
I listen to the trickling water
of the rill beneath and
rustling leaves above,
I plait the naked roots
writhing down into
brackish water
holding on to
the rutted slope
overgrown
[...]
rabbit ears
hacked off
petrified
in times past
[...]
bright orange flashes
thousands of sharp prongs
... my heart stands still ...
standing upright
regimented
one -- two -- three -- four
one -- two -- three -- four
marching
one – two – three – four
1 - 2 - 3 - 4
dispersed
... it takes my breath away ...
wrapped plastic corpses
frostbite-blue
cobwebs
floating downstream
I tremble

I fear
shrieking birds above
rumbling quakes below
screeching voices beyond
I shrink
I stiffen
I bear a thought
Should I
kneel down?
Weep?
One – two – three – four.
One - two - three.
The sky is high,
the hour late,
I cry and shut
the gate.

Ramallah

Sie ruft ihn, doch
er hört sie nicht –
unter den Trümmern.

Kein Laut, keine Stimme –
ihre Augen schließen sich
nach innen geöffnet.

Gedanken, Erinnerungen, Gefühle –
ein dicht gewebtes Netz voller
Täter und Opfer.

Bilder und Worte gefangen
ohne sich zu berühren –
sie trägt schwer.

Ein Fremder

Niemand konnte seine Stimme hören,
wenn er einsam und verlassen
durch die Gassen der Tauben lief,
bis er an den Rand des Wassers stieß.

Dort öffneten sich ihm die Ohren der
Stummen, und seine Zunge bewegte sich,
sie waren noch unvernetzt und unbefangen
hörten zu und hofften.

Jetzt ist seine Zunge eingeweckt
und aufbewahrt, jeder will sie sehen,
die unbewegt im Wunderglas nicht spricht, doch
manch Neugier auf der Durchreise wohl besticht.

Ein Fremder kann dies nur verstehen,
wenn seine eigene Zunge unbezweckt
die eingelegte Sprache spricht, und
keine Worte sinnlos bricht.

Auf der Suche

Auf der Suche
nach dem Mann mit den
drei Kirschkernen
im Sack
gehe ich durch das Tor
der Antike
und rufe

Gib mir ein Zeichen,
ich suche dich!

Die Antwort bleibt aus.
So gehe ich weiter,
setze mich an
den Rand der Welt
und warte.

SIMPLE ARITHMETIC

I am a box maker
twelve years old
and I make boxes
a hundred times my age
they say, every day.

I cannot count or read
very well because
they took me out of school
so that I could make three dollars
and twelve hundred boxes a day.

My mother is dead
my father makes six dollars
we all work in the same place
for the same man who owns all the
golden zipper fruits on the trees.

I have to leave now
because my best friend
waits at the gate for me.
Do you have a friend
waiting for you at the gate?

I dream that I'm a birdman
and one day I'll jump
from the tower and fly.
Think of me the next time
you bite into your sweet fruit.

NET-WORKING

You can be anything you want
... have anyone ...
walk the new bridges
to wealth and success
You can be hooked up
more inspired – less perspired
our fish are wriggling on the hook
happily caught things
don't worry be happy
you are safe
into the water – out of the water.

It's fun, isn't it!

We throw -- You jump!
We bait -- You swallow!
We pull -- You wriggle!
Our pool is open
24 hours a day.
Feel free and swim.
Relentlessly.
Continously.
Endlessly.
Bad fish turn gray,
rot and stink.
Good fish feed
and breed.
Stay on line.

HUMMING

Men and women
gazing
no one speaking
disasters repeating
children beseeching
humming top
men and women
jumping
from up high
living tower
power
shown
icons
alive

Speeches and justice
descending
no one mending
operations repeating
children weeping
humming top
martyrs and heroes
plunging
from up high
living tears
fears
known
icons
dead

Sons and daughters
missing
no one kissing
fingers kneading
bleeding scars
rumbling seats
foes and crows
burning
deep down low
killer stories
worries
blown
icons
born

The Day of Days gone
he opens the Book
of his father
waiting
for the son
of his son
rumbling
stumbling
humming
top.

For The Record

I
At 9:38
epiblast burst
on 9/11/2001
three membranes broke at
a 45-degree angle
by a regular 757
off regular schedule
gray-calcified ovum attacked
reversed bird's mission
blast-resistant glass
steel reinforcements
Kevlar mesh held
for 35 minutes
C Ring intact.

II
Terror
Counter
Terror
Attack
Terror
[...]

III
Silence
hatched
1/22/2002
Back to ...
let's roll
shave heads
sacrifice beards
spike faces with sweets
25 cents each

bids add up.
Some laugh!
Some cry!
Why?

IV
The golden buttercup
scorched in the heat
under turban fire.

V
Where is the road
to the cave
that returns from
the cave?
Where are they?
Hearing the
rat-tat-tatting
in the night
I fall asleep
tormented
survivor.

Amputiert

Keiner hat sie begraben und besungen,
die Täter, die Opfer, die Schuldigen, die Unschuldigen;
man hat
ihre Arme und Füße gesucht, ausgegraben,
auf Eis gelegt, fein säuberlich aufgelistet,
katalogisiert, abgeheftet, archiviert.
Nur so läßt sich Kummer anfassen, anschauen
numerierte Worte, statische Daten,
zählbare Hoffnungen.
Die Beine und Arme all der anderen sind
verschwunden, zerquetscht, verbrannt;
oder gar
abgehackt, in Steppenhitze verledert,
von wilden Tieren gefressen;
oder gar
abgeschossen, zerfetzt, zerfallen, verfault,
verscharrt worden,
oder gar
im ewigen Eis versargt
gewesen, nicht verwesen
doch vergessen.

Manche haben überlebt und gehen weiter
beinlos, armlos, mit und ohne Krücken,
vaterlos, mutterlos, mit und ohne Gebrechen.
Sie wollen in der Erinnerung leben,
Leere mit Phantomschmerzen füllen,
Sisyphusqualen schlucken können,
geformte Kügelchen aufrollen
wie Mistkäfer zum Überleben
in Leichenbäche springen
wie Fische zum Laichen.

Das Stöhnen der Toten dringt
nur an wenige Ohren.
Lärm amputiert.

FREI

frei
freitag
karfreitag
die erde bebte
und riß tiefe wunden
als das strömen verebbte
haben sie mich gefunden
erdblutverkrustet
krustenblutgeerdet
erdkrustenverblutet
verkrustete
bluterde
geerdete
blutkruste
verblutete
krustenerde
verkrustet
geerdet
verblutet

Am Meer

eingehüllt und bedeckt
herausgefallen aus der Zeit
gestrandet im warmen Sand
warte ich auf die Bilder
meiner Kindheit. Sie taumeln
im All, jagen an mir vorbei,
fallen zur Erde, verglühen.
Sternschnuppenwolkenzeit.

Muttermilch gerinnt
Worthülsen zerschellen
Schaumweiß versickert
im Sand der Erinnerung.
Ich warte auf das Meer.
Die Wasser der Flut
umhüllen mich
ich tauche ein
sinke tief
tiefer.

Das Meer
hat mich
wieder.

Warten

Einsam ist
der schwierige Akt
eine Fremde zu werden
das Innere nach Außen zu stülpen
damit die Sonne alte Wunden trocknet
die Wärme Grenzen auflöst
einfach warten können
die anderen machen lassen
sich selbst dem Anderssein hingeben
Bedeutungen neu setzen können
bis wieder umgestülpt werden muß
das Äußere zurück ins Innere
weitermachen
weiterleben
weitersein
einssein
sein

WAITING

How lonely is
the act of converting Yourself
into an unknown stranger –
as you turn your curled-up inside out
so that the sun can lick the oozing blood
and melt away your burning scars
be patient, then, learn to wait
let others be and do their work
your skin will thin and shed old folds
the rain shall clean the place from flaked old bits
before you turn your outside back in
the tear-stained friend is healed
then you step back and look anew
at meanings, dreams and worlds
just carry on with life
stride on and live
united with yourself
be you
just be
be one

Ach, Weisst Du

Ach, sagt die Mutter,
ohne dich wäre ich nie
an diesen Ort gekommen.
Und zum ersten Mal hört
die Tochter die Stimme
der Mutter ihren Namen
aussprechen.

Die Mutter hat den Namen
ihrer Tochter gerufen, die
seit Urzeiten unterwegs ist,
sich mitteilend fortbewegt.
Sie soll fürsprechen,
Worte gebären,
selbst tochterlos bleiben.

Ihr Name ist Emanuela.
Als Gesandte des Urnamens
soll sie verstanden werden.
Getrieben vom Geist des Wortes
sammelt und ordnet sie
Namen wie funkelnde Steine
aus fremden Ländern

bis sie erkennt:
Niemand will staunen!
Urgeschichten sind lange
abgeschafft und vergessen.
Man glaubt nicht mehr an
das geistig Schöne, sondern gibt
sich mit Vorlieben zufrieden. Töchter

wie Strandgut am Ufer aufgelesen
werden Coca oder Cola genannt.

Alfa soll sich ihre Locken rot färben,
weil man glaubt, es passe besser
zu ihrem heißen, roten Romeo.
Der Sichelmond strahlt muttermilchig
weiß im Licht der Schattensonne;

der lichtgrüne Specht pocht seine
Botschaft in den hohlen Baum;
die weiße Schneeblume bäumt sich
gegen die naßschwere, kalte Decke auf;
zartblaue Flügelschläge bedecken den Stein.
Das kleine Mädchen mit dem roten Rock
spielt mit sich allein auf dem steinigen Weg

das Kreuz-Spiel. Sie sagt nicht, warum
der rote Ball, der auf dem grauen Betonweg
aufspringen muß, um von ihr aufgefangen zurück
ins weiße Netz zu schnellen, diesen Namen trägt.
Sie lächelt nur und spielt weiter;
ihre Mutter erhebt sich von der Bahre
und geht zum Meer.

Rosemund

Ich kenne diesen Ort
der vielbenannten Steine
der zeitlosen Wiederkehr
sehr genau und doch
ist mir dieser eine
unvertraut geblieben.

ROSEMUND

Rosenzweige wachsen
links und rechts
aus dem steingekühlten Kelch,
Flügel, die sich öffnen wollen
und doch nicht fliegen können.

ROSEMUND

in Großbuchstaben
steht aufrecht, eingekerbt
gleichsam schwebend
zwischen Hier und Dort getragen
von einer einsamen Geraden
benanntes Leben
unverwandt
eingemeißelt
Rosenmensch
Rosenflügel ausgespannt
Rosenbank
Rosenstille abverlangt

[...]

Die Frau steht am Fenster
vergittert vor der blutrot
verschlungenen Dornenhecke
gefängnisprächtigen Rosenköpfen
und wartet; ihre Augen sind still;
sie schläft nicht. Sie wacht,
sie schichtet Lebensbilder um,
versteinerte Erinnerungshaufen.

Ihre Söhne sind verbrannt.
Auf dem Türstock stehen
in weißer Kreide
geschrieben
keine Namen.

11. 09. 2001

Und Es Rief

Und es rief mit lauter Stimme,
Kommt heraus!
Und die Toten kamen heraus,
Füße und Hände
umwickelt mit Seidenbändern,
Gesichter verhüllt.

Und die da rief,
nahm ihnen
die Verwicklungen ab,
öffnete die Bänder und
siehe da eingetaucht in Gold
die Gesichter strahlten.

Kalkweiße Hände
fingen an
zu putzen und zu waschen
und zu schälen.
Zartblaue Füße schritten
lautlos auf und ab bis sich

die Leiber küßten.
In inniger Umarmung
preßten sie sich aneinander
und verdichteten sich zu endlosen
Geschichten wie auffaltbare
Menschenfächer.

Und die Stimme rief ihr zu:
Schreib es heraus!
Und sie begann sich im Rhythmus
ihrer Hände und Füße
zu verdichten, aufzufächern
ins Unendliche,

ins immerwährende Ein-und
Auffalten feuchter Leiber.
Ausgewrungenes, abgerungenes
Lebenswasser
kondensiert zu Schreibwasser,
Blutschweißzeichen gedruckt
auf sinndurstige Lederhäute.

The Other Memorial Day

And on this Day
they remembered
the other battlefield.
They carried
their last remains
shrouded in black
out of the abyss
laid them to rest
onto a flatbed
special bier
covered with
fifty white roses.

I was not there.
Were you there?
Were you there, a man
of flesh and blood?

Were you there
when
they processed the
corpus mortale
the visible
the shrouded object
the body of steel?
They marched down
West Side Highway
drumming and singing
whistling and cheering
searching for
America the Beautiful.

He was there
repeating the same words

I don't deserve this
quietly crying
Why have you abandoned me.
He was there
the father
who had lost his son
in the flames
burnt to ashes
lost in grays
in the abyss
corpus immortale
the invisible
person shrouded in tears
the soul of man.
They remembered the doomed
lying on an empty bier.
They did not collect
the sun's ray.
They did not look at
the white birds
in the sky.

All theory, my friend,
is gray.

O Son of Power
for I know you already
why are you not hearing me?
I have been wounded like
you, an unyielding body
armored with steel
strong and invulnerable
before my foe forced me
against the rock

dashed me to the ground
before fear had taken
hold of me.
Remember me,
Listen to me.
Cygnus is my name.

The white bird perched
upon the white roses
and flapped its wings.
Everyone's eyes
were wide shut;
only the horse
riderless
turned its head
and neighed.

O son of peace
for I know you already
why are you not hearing me?
I have been wounded like
you, an unyielding spirit
tempted with fears
but armored with love.
They murdered me,
pierced me, mocked me,
wrapped my body in shrouds
laid me in the tomb,
they burnt me at the stake,
on the sedan, in the camps.
Yet the earth was shaken
and I rose from the dead.
Don't be afraid.

You have known me
since the beginning of time.
Remember me.
I am in you and you are in me.

The white bird perched
on her head, the head
of a stranger
and flapped its wings.
Shrouded in the veil
of the Unknown
she listened to
the voices.

Aphorismen

Leben heißt
sich zum Resonanzboden
der göttlichen Stimme zu machen.

Niemand muß
sich orginell gegen andere
abgrenzen, um Mensch zu werden.

Wer wie Atlas das Himmelsgewölbe
abgeben kann, ist den goldenen
Äpfeln näher.

Christus trug unser Kreuz wie Atlas
das seiner Brüder Prometheus und
Epimetheus auf sich nahm.

Einatmen-Ausatmen
füllt den Menschen als Menschen
aus, ohne ihn verbrauchen zu wollen.

Sprachkeime
sind verkapselte Geheimnisse,
die wie glitzernde Regentropfen zerplatzen,
wenn
sie aus dem Dunkel der Wolkenwand ins Licht
spiegelnder Oberflächen eintauchen.
Die Dämmerung weicht,
die Vögel zwitschern
und brüten ihre
Eier aus bis
sie
zerplatzen.

Popkornsprache ist
zum schnellen Verzehr geeignet.
Flauschig-weich und butterig-köstlich,
nichts zwischen den Zähnen
kein Biß nur Luft.

Wer sich keinen Zeitverlust
beim Sprechen und Schreiben
leisten kann, verdaut Sprachfastfood,
manscht und panscht,
verdünnt weiter
ohne Sinn.

Unter der Dusche
mit den Göttern perlen die Worte
auf der Haut ab bis sie eindringen
und ihr Tiefendasein
entfalten.

Ich Will Es Einfach Sagen

Die Zunge ist mir lahm;
auch sind die Hände taub,
die Füße müd' geworden
vom langen Laufen, tiefen Graben.
Noch muß ich viele Wälder roden,
die mir dein Wille aufgetragen
und unerschöpflich nagen, nagen.

Ich will es einfach sagen:

ich habe keinen Schatz gefunden
in fremder Erde noch auf trautem Herde;
trotz manch' unendlicher Beschwerde
ich leb' und werde.
Mein einzig' Erbe, das ich bei mir trage,
sind meine schrund'gen Narben
tief eingekerbt ins rohe Fleisch
vom Hacken, Fällen, Darben,
blutrot quellend auf dein Geheiß.

Ich will es einfach sagen:

die Zunge ist mir lahm,
die Händ' und Füß' mir müde,
die tiefste Wunde lang verschlossen.
Die einz'ge Weisheit, die ich fand
liegt in dir selbst verborgen
wohl Unbekannt benannt,
ins leise Innere verbannt.

Schicksal

Am Schicksal des anderen
mittragen
heißt sein Menschsein
auf-sich-nehmen
dem Schmerzensmann
ins Gesicht sehen
sich das Joch
der Menschwerdung
in die Haut einbrennen
wie ein Brandzeichen
mitwachsen lassen
langsam und bedächtig
schweigend
bis der Mensch
sich aufzulösen wagt
unter der Sonnenglut
wie ein Blitz
unter Grollen
zusammenbricht
der nächste Donner
zu rollen beginnt.
Dann wird es offenbar
wer Du
geworden bist.

SCHATTENFRAU

schattenfrau
du hast dich
gekrümmt und gewunden
müde geschunden warst tapfer
schließlich
abgebunden vom nabel archaischer lust

wer hat dich
getrieben
mit lava begossen
unter tosenden stürmen
erkalten lassen
unendlich
getragen und einsam vergraben

schwester
hörst du mich
du schattentaubes wesen
wie lange noch liegst du
erstarrt
bei den unsichtbar anderen in der totenwelt

frau
ich frage dich
wer hat deine augen verbunden
ohren versiegelt füße mit händen verriegelt
warum
die lippen verschlossen gar verstummen lassen

freundin
richte dich auf
recke dich dem sanften licht
entgegen wirf dein langes morgengrau
wenn
die neue zeit anbricht
auf die junge grünspitzige saat.

Woman Of The Shadow

Woman of the Shadow
who writhed with pain
You
Woman of Valor betoiled
wrapped in purple Throes
cut from the Omphalos
unknown.

Who hunted you,
poured lava over
You
ablaze, grown cold
against the storm-lashed gorge?
Who carried you
silently
to the tomb?

Sister,
Sojourner of the Dark,
can you hear me?
How long shall you
remain a frozen quest
a Shadow
in the Netherworld?

Woman,
Seeker of the Truth,
may I ask you?
Who pierced your eyes
who sealed your ears
nailed your feet onto
your hands?

Why
are your lips shut close
your Voices
barred from speaking
mute?

My Friend
wake up and rise
yearn for the gentle rays
and cast your slender morning-grays
as time has come
onto the tender, sprouting green
of the New Spring.

Once Upon A Time

I

Once upon a time
I lived within
your sacred walls
engulfed by streams
of gushing blood and
gently touching gales.
I loved you full of hope
since we were one.

II

Then time had come
for us to meet
outside the walls
to face the truth.
I wondered
who you *would* be
but you had dreamed
who I *should* be ...
a boy!
That very night
we burst in tears
and cried
from heart to heart
as lovers full of fear.
I was in need to eat and
you had breasts to feed
a girl!

III

Dear mother of mine!
Imagine
if I had been another boy born
raised and killed to be a hero-man?
Would you then love me more?
You know
I am a woman now
your daughter
called to be as free as
Snow-White's sisters are
delivered from my poisonous treat.

IV

We cannot change
the past of our failing dreams
yet our hands can join
in love and trust
and grant us peace
from womb to tomb
as you and me.

Das Kind

Sie sagen, das Kind sei nicht aus Glas,
weil niemand durch-sehen kann.

Sein Fleischhemd ist dicht gewirkt,
feinste Brokatfäden in zartestem Gewebe.
Ein schönes Kind.

Sie notieren sein Gewicht,
messen die Höhe und Tiefe seiner Statur.
Niemand weiß, wer es ist.

Nur es selbst weiß, wenn ...
seine Knochen vibrieren, wird es zu Glas.
Dann fällt das rotgoldene Brokathemdchen ab.

Es saugt sich das Mark aus den Knochen,
es läuft und läuft, markiert den Weg mit seinen Säften,
preßt seine Lebenssäule gegen die Schmerzensmauer.
Das Mark erkaltet in seiner Mundhöhle.
Das Kind friert und erstarrt.

Du mußt mehr essen,
ertönt die Stimme der Mutter.
Das Kind beginnt zu kauen, ernährt sich
vom eigenen Fett, verdaut sich selbst.
Gesichter verdichten sich zu Masken;
Erinnerungen zerrinnen zu Fettbildern;
Worte zerfließen und tropfen in den Sand.
Die Zunge reckt und streckt sich
wahr-lüstig nach vorne.

[...]

Sie hören das Zerspringen nicht.
Das Kind ist tot.
Das Kind lebt.

PORZELLANWEISS

Porzellanweiß
schön zurecht gemacht
zwischen makellosen Tüchern
eingebettet
bis der erste Schnitt
die weiße Glätte durchbrach
die Wunde fein säuberlich
aufgeklappt
Wundränder aufgerollt
wie Wickelstränge
verdickt und verstopft
mit Blutresten
ausgehauchte Zeitreste.

Da lag sie nun
die Schöne
porzellanweiß aufgebahrt
zwischen duftenden Blumen
hinter Glas wie Schneewittchen
vergraben bis die Maden kamen
emsig fressend
sich an ihrem Fette labten
sich ins tiefe Innere wagten
ihre Eier legten und
verschwanden.

Weisst Du, Warum?

Sie zieht den schwarzen Schleier
der Nacht zurück und gebiert die
Sonnenkinder des Tages.

Noch einmal berühren ihre Hände
das weiße Angesicht des Mondes
in dieser frühen Morgenstunde.

Die Ratsuchenden versammeln sich am
Fluß und waschen ihre Gesichter.
Das bunte Treiben der Fleischhändler

verblutet die Gassen. Tausende
von Opfertieren brüllen sich
keuchend den Berg hinauf.

Neue Qualen brennen sich in den
neuen Tag ein, Wund-Brandzeichen.
Weißt du, warum?

O Glücklicher Mensch!

Wie lange habe ich auf dich gewartet?
Schon seit Urzeiten weiß ich, daß du lebst,
doch erst jetzt spüre ich dein Bei-mir-sein.

Zeig mir den Quell deiner Kraft,
den Pfad des Lichtes, auf dem du ausgreifst,
du weißes Lichtpferd.

Laß mich deine Sonnenflügel anlegen,
die dich aus der Asche emporhoben,
du neugeborener Feuervogel.

Gewähr mir tröstende Anlehnung
inmitten traurigwüster Verödung
du grünender Totenpfahl.

O glücklicher Mensch!
Wirf deinen aschgrauen Mantel
auf die Erde, laß ihn zerfallen.

Vater

Das Himmelreich
liegt dir zu Füßen.
Gehe nur voran
und scheue dich nicht.

Gelbe Schlüsselblumen
und weiße Windröschen
säumen den Bergpfad.
Gehe nur voran
und warte nicht auf mich.

Ich muß das Erdreich noch
kräftig wässern, junge Pflänzchen
setzen und die Früchte ernten,
bevor der Boden sich härtet, die
Sonne kälter wird, mein Vater.
Sorge dich nicht,
ich komme nach.

Ich schloß die Augen,
hörte sein Röcheln nicht mehr,
schlief nicht.
Der Braten hörte auf zu brutzeln wie damals
als der Koch dem Küchenjunge keine Schelle gab,
als das Mädchen sich an der Spindel stach,
und das Geheimnis sich erfüllte.

Meine Hand griff nach einem Halt
und gewahrte die Rosen auf den Perlen;
wie Rosen schöner sind als Dornen,
sind Liebeslieder schöner als
Totenlieder, die ich nicht
schreiben
kann.

Die Brotkrume

Sie zogen den Esel durch die Gassen
und sangen ihre Lieder,
die Mädchen in weißen Kleidern vorweg
als Blumenkinder,
dann die Buben in blauen Hosen
als Fahnenträger.
Der graue Esel schwieg geduldig
gezogen auf Rollen.

Sie sangen die alten Lieder,
die sie schon immer gesungen hatten
und niemand fragte sich,
warum dem so sei.

Tücher wurden ausgebreitet,
das Mahl zubereitet und gegessen,
dann sorgfältig ausgeschüttelt.
Die Brotkrumen gebührten
den Vögeln des Himmels.
Eine Krume lag noch lange dort
bis der Schnee sie zugedeckt.

Der Kinderchor verstummte,
die Alten gingen weg,
die Vögel starben aus.
Nur die eine vereiste Brotkrume taute
wieder auf, die Samen auf ihrer Rinde von
damals konnten sich mit Wasser vollsaugen,
in die Erde fallen
und anfangen zu sprießen.

Ahnend

Meine Lider waren noch verschlossen,
als ich sie kommen sah.
Ich wich zurück und ahnte doch
wie nah sie waren.

Der erste Schnitt –
Ich wehre mich, bäume mich auf;
das Netz hält mich nicht mehr,
es bricht der Damm und ich, die Fluten ...

Meine Lippen waren stumm, verriegelt,
als ich sie sprechen hörte,
ich krümmte mich und schreckte gar,
schon ahnend, daß ich machtlos war.

Der zweite Schnitt –
Ich verlier' den Kampf und spüre sie,
ergeb' mich stimmlos ihren Händen,
ihren Zangen, die nach mir langen.

Mein Lebenssinn war noch versiegelt,
als ich schön umwickelt, wohl geformt
als Fremdling angekommen war
nicht ahnend, wer und wo ich war.

Der letzte Schnitt –
sie ziehen mich hoch und ich
ergreif' zum ersten Mal das Wort im Zorn
beginne gegen den Tod anzuschreien.

Aufwachen

aufwachen und lachen.
in den Tag hineinhören,
die Augen öffnen,
die Sonne sehen;

endlose Goldfäden
ziehen durch den
Frühnebel
smaragdgrün
saphirblau
rubinrot;

Juwelen brechen ab
erneuern sich
schmerzlos
gleichsam
lautlos;

aufwachen und wachen,
in den Tag hineingehen,
ganz sachte die Augen
schließen und
nach innen
hören.

Sophia

She gave birth to a beautiful girl and said,
Welcome to my heart, Sophia.

She walked the way of all mothers.
Her Story of Wisdom was born.

Sophia told her daughters, granddaughters and
great-granddaughters the Truth about Beauty
and they kept it in their hearts.

Then time came to speak no more.

Closing her eyes she said in a whisper,
Remember me.

[...]

She gave birth to beautiful ideas and said,
Welcome to my life.

She walked into the jungle of lush reveries
and colorful ecstasies.
Poems and paintings were born and multiplied.

Listening to her own voice,
she called the Voice of all Voices.
No one answered.

She called Sophia by name
and embarked on the way of all mothers.
She was alone on this abandoned, stony road.
She was cold.

Then time came to walk no more.

She closed her eyes and sat down.
She re-membered her story;
it had survived yet unknown and untold.

[...]

She gave birth to a beautiful girl and said,
Welcome to my heart, Sophia.

Erinnerungslied

Erinnerungsspuren
Ungeweinte Tränen
Zeigen und Zulassen
Verzittert und Verwittert
Getreten und Gequält
vergangene Tage
wegdenken.

Erinnerungsräume
Verlorene Gesichter
Körperwände
Glastische
mit sieben Tellern
Haupt-Nebenrollen
wegschieben.

Erinnerungsbäume
Verweste Blätter
Wurmige Rinden
Zerfressene
Lieblingsschäfer
mit Hund
aufgehängt.

Erinnerungskuren
Abgestellte Schmerzen
Vergessen und Verlassen
Zwitschern
Glaswände verflüssigen
Einverleibte
abgehängt.

WEITER

Ich fühle mich wohl unter ihnen,
Rose Lee, Michie, Kenneth und John,
schweigend inmitten ihrer eingekerbten Existenz.

Würde ich MATTER oder VOGEL heißen wollen?
Der Wind spielt mit meinem Haar,
als ob Zephyr mir schmeicheln wolle
mit seiner luftkalten Zunge.

Wie tief muß man graben, um den Mahl-stein zu heben?

Es schreit aus mir heraus:
Grab weiter!
Grab weiter!

Wo weiter? Wie weiter? Warum weiter?

Und Nathaniel bläst seine Backen auf
wie ein Eichhörnchen im Winter.
Sein Augen starren mich an.

Wo hat er seine Samen vergraben?

Sie klagen: sein Mahl-stein zer-brach zu früh.
11. September 2001
Sie sagen: sein Stein-bild ist doch so schön.
30. Mai 1980

Ich frage: Wo finde ich dich?
16. November 2001

Weiter!

Burgermeister*

Sie sind angekommen.
Die Fahnen wehen.
Köpfe recken und strecken sich,
die Panzerluke öffnet sich,
ein schwarzer, helmgeschützter
Panzerkopf kommt hervor.
Alle starren und warten
gebannt auf den nächsten Akt
bis er ruft:

Burgermeister!
Burgermeister!

Das Mädchen mit dem goldenen Haar
reißt die Augen auf, bewegt sich nicht,
hört wachsam hin:

Where is the mayor?
Do you speak English?

Ihr langer Zopf schwingt gleichmäßig
hin und her
wie ein Uhrenpendel.

Do you speak English?

Die stille Sprachlose hebt den Kopf
mit leicht geöffnetem Mund,
der dicke, blonde Zopf bleibt stehen.
Zeitlosigkeit bricht an.
Sie senkt den Kopf, schließt
Augen und Lippen,
zeigt Sprachlosigkeit an

*aus: *Des Mädchens Wundersinn*

bis orakelhafte, rhythmische Laute
aus ihrem Mund hervorquellen,
ein Sprachwildwasser sprudelt.

Hiccup, hiccup, go away!
Come again another day;
Hiccup, hiccup, when I bake,
I'll give to you a butter cake.

Köpfe drehen und wenden sich,
der Panzerkopf taucht ab
in den dunklen, schalltoten Raum,
die Panzerluke schließt sich wieder,
betroffenes Schweigen folgt
bis sich die Luke abermals öffnet.
Ein weißes, behelmtes Gesicht
taucht auf, taucht ab;
ein schwarzes, behelmtes Gesicht
taucht auf, taucht ab.
Ein Auf und Ab
Erscheinungsbilder
ein Kasperltheater.
Das blauäugige Mädchen mit dem
langen, blonden Zopf
beginnt zu lachen,
die Panzerköpfe beginnen zu lachen,
alle Köpfe beginnen zu lachen.

Die Schallmauer ist durchbrochen,
der zu lange angehaltene Atem
sprengt die aufgeblähten Wangen
und ein brustendes Lachen
bahnt sich seinen Weg ins Freie.

Der Kasperl ist immer lustig und
hat immer recht,
deshalb können, müssen, sollen
alle lachen und froh sein.
Er liebt seine Frau ebenso
wie die Königin ihren König liebt

und ruft:
Seid's alle da?
Jahhh!
antwortet das Mädchen.

Nur
vor dem Teufel und dem Polizisten
haben die Leute Angst,
weil sie nicht aus Frohsinn lachen
und handeln.
Der eine mit den Hörnern auf dem Kopf
verspricht Macht und Ehre,
wenn man sich ihm zu Füßen wirft;
der andere mit dem Helmhut
verspricht keine Macht und Ehre
und trotzdem muß man sich ihm beugen.

Und wo bleibt der arme Mohr?

Das Mädchen ängstigt sich
und rennt in den Stall
hinter dem Haus.

Noch nie
in ihrem kleinen Leben
hat sie Panzer gesehen.
Noch nie
in ihrem kleinen Leben

hat sie Panzerköpfe gesehen.
Noch nie
in ihrem kleinen Leben
hat sie solche Angst gehabt.
Noch nie
in ihrem kleinen Leben
ist ihr Herz so still gestanden.

Sie will zu Blessie,
ihrer Freundin,
sie ganz nah an sich herandrücken,
um ihren Herzschlag zu spüren.
Blessie lebt ihr eigenes Auf und Ab.
Nicht Minuten oder Stunden,
Tage oder Wochen,
Monate oder Jahre,
Krieg oder Frieden,
Leben oder Tod,
Arbeit und Freizeit
zählen in ihrem Leben.
Sie folgt stillschweigend
Bedürfnissen und Nöten,
pendelt ihre Stimmungen
mit dem Schweif aus.

Blessie ist
eine schwarz-weiß gescheckte
Kuh
mit großen, runden Augen
und einem Euter
voller Milch.
Die Glocke um ihren Hals
braucht sie eigentlich nicht
zum Überleben,
eher die anderen,

um ihre Glockenschläge
zu hören.
Sie brauchen
Blessies Gezeitenschläge.
(Blessies are soft
something to touch
something to hold onto
something warm and moist.)
Und die Männer steigen aus
ihren Panzerluken.
Einer nach dem anderen
verläßt die sichere Höhle.
Schwarze und weiße Männer in
grünbraun gescheckter Kleidung.
Ihre Beine sind müde.
Langsam schreiten sie in Richtung
Haus.

Sie sehnen sich nach Ruhe,
brauchen Betten.
Vielleicht auch Butterkuchen
mit Milch.

Die Bauersfrau ist in der Küche
und feuert den Ofen an
mit einem traurigen Lied
auf den Lippen.

Maikäfer flieg,
dein Vater ist im Krieg.
Die Mutter ist in Pommerland,
Pommerland ist abgebrannt.
Maikäfer flieg.

Der Bauer ist abwesend.
Vermißt, gewesen, verwest?

Die Bauersfrau mit dem
verwittert-verwelkten Gesicht
lebt schon lange alleine,
mit dem Kind, dem Mädchen
mit dem goldenen Haar.

Die Panzermänner treten in die Stube,
legen Schokolade, Zigaretten
und Kaugummi auf den Tisch.
Die Bauersfrau blickt auf die Gaben.
Sie versteht die wortlose Geste
der Fremden.
Dann durchsuchen sie das Haus,
steigen hinab in den Keller
hinauf in den Speicher,
öffnen alle Türen,
Schubladen und Schachteln.
Sie finden nicht, was sie suchen
bis einer die oberste Kammer
betritt.
Die anderen folgen nach, bis jeder
den Fuß ins kalkweiße
Gewölbe
gesetzt hat
Das Türschloß klickt ein.
Die Männer bleiben.

Die Bauertrau geht zum Kind.
Beide schlafen im Stall
mit Blessie

bis das kleine Mädchen mit
den goldenen Zöpfen aufwacht.

Der Mond hat sich noch kaum versteckt,
Blessie, die Kuh, schnaubt noch laut im Traum,
aber die dünnen Spinnenbeine des Kindes wollen stehen,
wollen gehen, die Sonne sehen.
Ein Strumpfträger ist in der Nacht gerissen,
das linke Strumpfbein hängt lose herab
wie die faltige Haut einer Schildkröte.
Die buntbestickte weiße – eher grauweiße – Bluse
mit den kurzen, gerafften Ärmchen ist zerknittert.
Mit feinsinnigen Händen streicht das Kind
ihren blauen Rock glatt und zupft
vereinzelte Strohhalme aus
den Faltentälern.
Neugierig und frohgemut
stapft sie ins Freie,
verläßt den Stall,
geht zum Haus.
Sie singt.

Kommt und laßt uns tanzen, springen,
kommt und laßt uns fröhlich sein.
Froh zu sein, bedarf es wenig,
und wer froh ist, ist ein König.
Will ich in mein Gärtlein gehn,
will mein Zwiebeln gießen,
steht ein bucklig Männlein da,
fängt gleich an ...

Die letzten Worte bleiben dem Kind
im Hals stecken;
zwischen den gelben Osterglocken

im Gärtlein steht der Panzer.
Sie hatte ihn vergessen.

Sie singt weiter.
... fängt gleich an zu niesen.
Will ich in mein Küchel gehen,
will mein Süpplein kochen,
steht ein bucklig Männlein da,
hat das Töpflein brochen.

Sie freut sich.
Osterglocken
werden
Weihnachtsglocken
gleichen
Kuhglocken
werden
Kirchenglocken.

Und sie singt.
Alles schläft, einsam wacht
nur das traute, hochheilige Jahr,
holden Mädchen schlägt die rettende
Stund, tönt es laut von fern und nah
vom Himmel hoch da komm ich her
und bring euch eine gute Mär...

Das Kind geht singend durch die Haustür
Will ich in mein Stüblein gehn,
will mein Müslein essen,
steht ein bucklig Männlein da,
hat's schon halber gessen.
Die Holzdielen knarzen morgenlahm
unter seinen zaghaften Schritten.
Langsam und vorsichtig steigt

es die Treppe hoch.
Will ich in mein Kämmerlein,
will mein Bettlein machen,
steht ein bucklig Männlein da,
fängt gleich an zu lachen.
Das Mädchen will sich neue
Strumpfhalter holen.
Es liebt seine Kuh über alles
und trägt den Stallgeruch
porentief in die Haut eingedrungen
stolz durchs ganze Haus.
Die Panzermänner
mit den Metallhüten
müssen sich doch irgendwo
versteckt haben?
Will ich in mein Keller gehn,
will mein Weinlein zapfen,
steht ein bucklig Männlein da,
tut mir'n Krug wegschnappen.
Sind die Männer vielleicht
über den sieben Bergen
bei den sieben Zwergen
mit Schneewittchen,
der schönsten Prinzessin,
die von ihrer Stiefmutter gehaßt
und fast getötet wurde,
wo alle Flüsse ins Meer laufen
am anderen Ende der Welt?
denkt das Mädchen so vor sich hin
und kommt der Tür
zur obersten Kammer
immer näher.
Ob es auch schwarze Zwerge gibt?
Tragen alle Zwerge Zipfelmützen?

Oder vielleicht gibt es Zwerge
mit Metallhüten oder
tragen sie gar Turbane?

Und als das Mädchen
singend und nachdenkend
sich über ihre buckligen Gedanken
wundert
ist sie oben angekommen.
Die Tür
öffnet sich
von alleine.
Ein ungewohnter,
ja beißender Geruch
unähnlich dem zitronigen
Limonengeruch, den das Kind so liebt,
läßt es niesen.
Seine Mutter versteckte früher immer
frisch getrocknete Lavendelblüten
zwischen der Wäsche.
Aber der Lavendel blüht
schon lange nicht mehr
und die Limonen ...?

Alle Schubläden stehen offen, gleichen
hungrigen Mäulern mit vorgeschobenen,
fletschenden Zähnen.
Der Boden ist gedeckt mit weißen Tüchern,
langen Nachthemden
ausgespreizten Unterhosenbeinen,
ausgewalzten Menschentüchern
flach und leblos
zwischen Chaos und Leere
sich windend.

Das goldene Gelb des Eies
gegen die Decke geworfen,
ist vertropft
zu Tropfgelbstein
erstarrt.
Seiner eigenen Schwerkraft gehorchend
rankt sich Tropfgold um
die Häute der weißen Hüllenmenschen,
raffinierte Tätowierungen
die sich zwischen aufgeschichteten,
fedrigweißen Schneeflockenhäufchen
aus aufgeschlitzten Federbetten hervorquellend,
eingenistet haben.
Anfaßbares, Stoffe, Materialien können
nicht wegschmelzen, verschwinden.
Wer sind die Akrobaten?
Sind die Metallhutmänner
aus dem Panzer
das gewesen?

Das kleine Mädchen lacht
in sich hinein und singt
die letzte Strophe seines Liedes,
während es beginnt auf-zu-räumen,
Ordnung zu schaffen.
Will ich an mein Bänklein gehn,
will ein bißchen beten,
steht ein bucklig Männlein da,
fängt gleich an zu reden:

Liebes Kindlein, ach, ich bitt,
*bet fürs bucklig Männlein mit.**

**Das bucklige Männlein* aus: *Des Knaben Wunderhorn*

Postscriptum

The war was over but not yet.
The Burgermeister was dead.
This night everyone fell asleep
not knowing
the name of the other,
not knowing
the story of the other,
not knowing
the fate of the other,
of the country,
of the world
but
hoping
to live.

Wie Oft

Wie oft bin ich diese Wege gegangen

habe die Schritte gezählt
den Atem gespürt
den Klang meiner Füße im Ohr

schaute ich
vorwärts, seitwärts
nach links und rechts
wohin die anderen der Welt
marschierten

bis der Nagel meinen Fuß durchbohrte
und das Messer meine Hand durchstieß.

Ich hielt an
und schaute neu.
Rückwärts, seitswärts
nach Ost und West
in die Leere hinein.

Mein Augenlicht wandte sich nach innen
mein Ohr gewahrte den Klang

bis meine Füße vibrierten
zarte Wurzeln durch mein Schuhwerk brachen
auf der Suche nach dem Lied der Erde.

Das Lied der vielen Meilen
strömte durch mich wie eine Melodie;
ich bin durch mich hindurch
geflossen und

hier steh' ich nun
soweit mich meine Füße trugen
allein
wach
und
freue mich.

And the Gray-Eyed Old Woman Says Remember

Eingekerkert
Imprisoned within
Come to me and show
Ihr Fleisch an Knochen
They found a young man
The Dead won't cry
They were born and died
Senem Kus
Kein Baum erinnert mehr
Vater - Mutter
Löse die Klammern aus meinem Fleischhemd
It rumbles and quakes
Shuttered
When I was young I was told
Weißt du, daß ich ein Kristall bin?
A Word
Eine Hand voll
Alone
How comes it
He coiled up
They came and stayed
The Unseen is hunted like a bird
Dead
Er geht
Sie öffnen und schließen
Die weiße Made frißt sich durch
Call him Mohammed, the young man
Why are you hanging in the closet, little boy?
Brother, is this the place of all places?
I am b-r-o-k-e-n
One Son says
Standing on the bridge
Sie ruft ihn, doch
Niemand konnte seine Stimme hören

Auf der Suche
I am a box maker
You can be anything you want
Men and Women
At 9:38
Amputiert
Frei
Eingehüllt und bedeckt
Einsam ist
How lonely is
Ach, sagt die Mutter
Ich kenne diesen Ort
Und es rief mit lauter Stimme
And on this Day
Leben heißt
Die Zunge ist mir lahm
Am Schicksal des anderen
Schattenfrau
Woman of the Shadow
Once upon a time
Sie sagen, das Kind sei nicht aus Glas
Porzellanweiß
Sie zieht den schwarzen Schleier
Wie lange habe ich auf dich gewartet?
Das Himmelreich
Sie zogen den Esel durch die Gassen
Meine Lider waren noch verschlossen
Aufwachen und lachen
Sie gave birth to a beautiful girl and said
Erinnerungsspuren
Ich fühle mich wohl unter ihnen
Sie sind angekommen
Wie oft bin ich diese Wege gegangen
Eingekerkert

And when they arrived
they were amazed
asking many questions.
When the noise of opinions settled
they listened and understood.

Life hums
Man speaks
Death rattles

Without wind there is no movement
without breath there is no sound
without spirit there is no life

tibia books invite readers
to breathe
to pause
to play

tibia books believe in
meaningful words
melodic voices
maieutic beauty

tibia books play the flute
for seekers
for strangers
for storytellers

tibia books are not replaceable;
they are unique treasures
to be gently treated
full of poetic life
to be shared.